FROM WHENCE WE CAME...

A FUN POLITICAL EDUCATIONAL CONVERSATION

A GIFTED & MAGICAL 95% BOOK

By Juliette Adams

ISBN 978-1-68524-778-2

DEDICATION

To my daughter, Terica Adams, a contextual space thinker and millennial leader who seeks knowledge in unknown areas. She is an emerging player in the emerging space industry with the responsibility to empower her generation through increasing their awareness that innovation and creativity are in the power of understanding from Whence We Came.

To all educators who understand the importance of tracing and teaching historical events for meaningful present-day solutions. Especially the fantastic Summer 2021 multinational educator team members from Asia, the Caribbean, Europe, Latin America, and the United States.

TABLE OF CONTENTS

NEWS FLASH 1

INTRODUCTION 2

THE JOURNEY BEGINS 6

EXPLORING THE LEGISLATIVE PROCESS 10

HIGHLIGHTING THE U.S. CONSTITUTION........................19

IN THE DRIVER'S SEAT... YOUR TURN.............................27

APPENDIX: PERSONAL POLITICAL WORKSHEET................31

APPENDIX: LETTER WRITTEN TO REPRESENTATIVE ED ROYCE (CA) ..33

APPENDIX: LETTER TO SECRETARY OF EDUCATION ARNE DUNCAN..34

APPENDIX: LETTER RECEIVED FROM REPRESENTATIVE TOM DAVIS (VA) 37

PORTFOLIO OF SAMPLE CAMPAIGN TOOLS FOR 2016 OHIO SENATE RACE 38

    7-DAY MESSAGE CALENDAR SAMPLE 41

    MEDIA ADVISORY 43

    TALKING POINTS: SENATOR ROBERT PORTMAN 45

    EXTRACT OF PORTMAN MESSAGE BOX 48

    PRESS RELEASE 50

    NEWS STORY 52

    SPEECH...55

    OP-ED FOR THE DAYTON DAILY NEWS 58

REFERENCES 61

ABOUT THE AUTHOR...63

SUPPORTING FRAMEWORK FOR THE SERIES 65

For the first time, the Washington Post reported that the US had been added to the list of "backsliding democracies," as evaluated by the International Institute for Democracy and Electoral Assistance (IDEA) Global State of Democracy 2021 report. The key indicators cited were the restrictions on free speech and the weakening of the rule of law. The International IDEA is an intergovernmental organization that supports sustainable democracy worldwide.

United States government shutdown:
October 6, 1990 - October 8, 1990: H.W. Bush Administration
United States government shutdown:
December 16, 1995 - January 6, 1996: Clinton Administration
United States government shutdown:
October 1, 2013 - October 17, 2013: Obama Administration
United States government shutdown:
December 22, 2018 - January 25, 2019: Trump
Administration

A U.S. government shutdown occurs when the legislative and executive branches fail to pass temporary or permanent legislation to finance the government for its next fiscal year (October 1 - September 30). During the 2018-2019 shutdown, government offices and buildings were closed, employees did not perform federal services, and workers did not receive a paycheck (even though some were designated as essential workers and were still required to perform their job responsibilities). Why does this occur? Have Congressional leaders become fiscally inefficient? Can you imagine failures of this magnitude occurring in private business with the same frequency?

It is hardly difficult to understand why voters are highly dissatisfied with the country's direction. A June 2021 Gallup poll measuring public opinion on the country's direction reported that only 35% of respondents were satisfied with the direction of the U.S., while 63% of respondents were dissatisfied. A February 2021 Gallup poll measuring whether respondents viewed their political party favorably had even more dismal results. While 48% of Democratic respondents had favorable opinions of the Democratic Party, only 37% of Republican respondents had favorable views for their political party.

The U.S. democracy is at a crossroads, evident by the January 6, 2021 insurrection on Capitol Hill when an organized group of individuals claimed they were challenging the legitimacy of the November 2020 elections. This incident is an example of a grassroots movement choosing to use violent confrontation, even though the U.S. has democratic political institutions to address the legitimacy of elections. This example clearly illustrates that the democratic process is in immediate need of extensive repair and rebuilding. Citizens and voters must unlearn harmful messaging about their insignificance in the political process and relearn one of their most important roles as citizens in a democratic republic so that incidents like the January 6 insurrection never recur. Though politicians, community leaders, and educators share responsibility for educating individuals on their power within the political system, it is seldom done. The onus of acquiring a robust political education is on the individual. Therefore, citizens must seek civic education with increased attention to economic equity, justice, and greater community involvement.

This book is written as a conversation between two individuals on the primary responsibility of a citizen and how the U.S. government functions. In an anxious environment where politics has terrifying connotations for the average citizen, satire can be an effective and lighthearted way to break down this complex and confusing topic. Thus, you take the driver's seat in an entertaining and facilitated active learning environment.

The conversational approach addresses the human need to be heard. It uses a "listening and talking" format to reduce feelings of alienation, confusion, and anxiety by many who want to act but do not know how. Humor is used to heighten the awareness of the average grassroots voter to their incredible power and inalienable rights as decreed by the Founding Fathers. Additionally, readers can align themselves with a character featured in this satirical conversation and confidently navigate through the political journey.

On this journey, you will meet two characters. Dux (Latin for guide) is a political consultant who loves educating voters on the political system and their duty as citizens.

Discipulus (Latin for student) is an auto mechanic who seeks to become more educated and involved in the political system. He wants to learn how to leverage his political power to make a substantial difference for himself and his community by taking political science lessons from Dux.

Thank you for your participation as we take off on a journey to experience the basic structure of government, its function, and citizens' responsibility. Please enjoy the satirical journey!

Dux: Do you realize that most Americans are mystified about the government and their responsibility as citizens? They know little about the nation's fundamental political organization. Even though there has been a greater focus on the electoral process, most Americans are clueless about the Electoral College. It remains one of the biggest political mysteries. Listen, politics does not end on election day. It continues 365 days a year. History matters. From where did we come? How did we get here?

Discipulus: Please do not get too intellectual with me, Dux. From my experience and observations, political intellectualism equals inactivity. I am an ordinary registered voter. Based on their behaviors, I think those guys sitting in Congress and the White House are doing their own thing...

Dux: Let me begin. A government, regardless of what you think of it, is essential to society. One definition of government is a formal institution through which land

and people are ruled. It could be as simple as a tribal council as in Native American society or as complex as the constitutional monarchy seen in the United Kingdom and Japan. I can understand your dismay; that is the general mood of the country. Based on a May 2021 Statista poll, the approval rating for the U.S. Congress was 31%.

However, let me highlight that women also make up the U.S. government. So, it is not only "those guys." The frustration and disappointment you feel should also be directed to women who hold elected leadership positions.

Now for greater detail. There are three parts, also known as branches, of the government:

1. The Executive branch includes the president and vice-president, cabinet members, and the leaders of independent agencies. The executive branch is responsible for carrying out and executing federal laws. This branch typically becomes your focus every four years due to the presidential election.
2. The Judicial branch is the arm of government that interprets laws through the federal courts, with the Supreme Court as the highest court in the land. The Supreme Court has nine judges and decides the most monumental cases. This branch does not make headlines as much as the other branches; however, it gets the most attention when new judges are to be appointed

and when very high-profile or controversial
cases are debated. It is a meaningful privilege
for a president to elect judges to the Supreme
Court since it is a job for life.
3. The Legislative branch, typically called
Congress, makes national laws. It comprises the
House of Representatives and the Senate. Now
that is where your initial interest should begin.
Congress is the branch where most of your
participation will occur.

Discipulus: If I visualize the government like a tree with
three branches, no wonder the tree seems to be in
such a bad shape! Very interesting. What about the
judges? Do they experience job insecurity?

Dux: No, and that was entirely intentional so they would
be less swayed by political pressure or the fleeting
trends of the moment.

Discipulus: I suppose that makes sense, although it sounds
a little too cushy for my liking. Would you please
explain the process of becoming a Supreme Court
justice?

Dux: Gladly. First, the president makes the nomination.
Then the Senate votes to confirm the individual.
However, there can be obstacles in the actual process.
Sometimes if the Senate majority leader is of a
different party from the president, they can refuse to
put forward the nominee and stall the process. That is
precisely what happened to Judge Merrick Garland.

Though nominated by Democratic President Barack Obama, Senate Majority Leader Mitch McConnell, a Republican, refused to consider his nomination for 293 days. He stated that the Supreme Court justice would be chosen by the next president almost one year later. Yet when circumstances arose that created a vacancy on the Supreme Court less than two months before the 2020 presidential election, Senator McConnell chose to push through Amy Coney Barrett's confirmation 30 days after her nomination by President Donald Trump.

Discipulus: Ah! Power and control rule politics. For the Republicans, it was obstruction rather than the people's business. With all those intelligent politicians, I wonder why the Democrats could not develop clever, innovative, and creative ideas to override the Republican strategy? If the people were politically empowered, it would have changed the whole picture, and who knows, Judge Garland would have been a Supreme Court justice instead of the U.S. Attorney General.

Congresswoman Shirley Chisholm

Discipulus: Can you tell me about the legislative branch? Is it part of a legislative tree?

Dux: In a way. The legislative branch gets broken into two parts: the House of Representatives and the Senate. The House has 435 members, and this number is based on the total population in a specific geographic location. The Senate is comprised of 100 members, two per state regardless of the total population. I know you would be surprised to learn there are 535 elected officials in the legislature relative to the number of bills passed. It is because one part of the legislative branch could stall the passage of a law for any reason, justified or unjustified.

One example can be seen with the third stimulus package during the COVID-19 pandemic that gave individuals $1,400 from March to December 2020. The Republican majority Senate in the 116th Congress opposed the bill and chose not to vote on it. As 2020 was an election year, the composition of the Senate in 2021 changed to tilt in favor of the Democrats. The bill was later brought to vote and passed with a 51 – 50 vote (the Democratic vice-president served as the tiebreaker).

Discipulus: Well, I need to evaluate the competency of my leaders, so I will know how to vote! It is serious business for me; the more I become enlightened.

Dux: Now, let me share how decisions are made. The legislative process is very rule-oriented. Legislators must follow strict procedures and guidelines!

Discipulus: Hmm… Interesting!!!

Dux: Anytime you want Congress to act, it must be presented in the form of a bill or resolution submitted officially by a senator, a representative to the clerk of the House, and referred to the appropriate committee for deliberation.

No floor action on any bill can occur until the committee with jurisdiction deliberates on it. During deliberations, the committee typically forwards the bill to one of the subcommittees, which may hold hearings, listen to expert testimony, and amend the proposed legislation before referring the bill to the full committee for consideration.

Believe this Discipulus, the committee or subcommittee can choose to do little or nothing with a bill and prevent it from leaving the committee.

Discipulus: My goodness… Is that what our elected officials working for us sometimes do? Nothing! They really have a field day.

Dux: Listen carefully. In a typical Congressional session, 85 to 90 percent of the legislation is not taken up. Sometimes a resolution may be frivolous, but other times it could be a bill meant to address a prevalent economic issue. For example, the Paying a Fair Share Act of 2012, also known as the "Buffett Rule," would have ensured that individuals earning more than $2 million paid a minimum 30 percent effective federal tax rate. Those earning between $1 million and $2 million would have their taxes phased in. This bill was not moved forward from the committee to be voted on by the full Senate.

Between January 3, 2019 to January 3, 2021, the 116th Congress enacted 344 laws and passed 714 resolutions. If we look further, 746 pieces of legislation received only an in-committee vote, with nothing happening afterward. There were 24 resolutions that failed to pass, and nine bills were vetoed without an override. That leaves us with 14,764 bills that never received a vote. For additional perspective, only eleven percent of legislation was acted upon. It just shows you the power of the Congressional committee system to determine how much legislation gets through to the larger group.

Discipulus: My goodness. I wonder what was contained in that 85 to 90 percent of bills. Maybe those are the bills Congress needs to pass.

Dux: If you visit www.congress.gov, you will find federal legislative information freely available to the public.

Discipulus: Such freedom and liberty we have in this great nation! There must be greater grassroots awareness and action to maximize our insight in the legislative process. I will certainly now be a congress.gov fan.

Dux: In continuing with the legislative process, a debate ensues after the committee allows a resolution or bill to go to the larger group. Generally, the party leadership in the House has total control over the discussion. However, the U.S. Senate is unique among the world's legislative bodies for its commitment to "unlimited debate." Once given the floor, a senator may speak as long as they wish unless an extraordinary majority vote ends the debate. This practice is known as a filibuster. On several occasions, senators have used the filibuster to prevent legislation they opposed.

Discipulus: Oh, they have their politics within instead of taking care of the people.

Dux: Let's call it the politics of politics. Through a filibuster, small minorities or even individuals in the

Senate can force the majority to give in to their demands.

Discipulus: Ok, so what if a filibuster fails and a bill gets passed by both parts of Congress?

Dux: When adopted by the House and Senate, a bill goes to the president, who may sign it into law or veto it.

Discipulus: What is a veto?

Dux: The veto means rejecting the bill by not signing it into law. However, a presidential veto is overridden by a two-thirds vote in the House and the Senate. Often a president backs down from a veto threat if they believe that Congress has the votes to override the veto.

Discipulus: Now tell me, what is the deciding factor in how Congressional leaders make decisions? Do they respond to the views of the constituents?

Dux: That is a touchy point because members of Congress want to be reelected. So, the views of constituents can substantially impact those decisions. Yet, believe it or not, the majority of the constituents do not know the policies their representatives support.

Discipulus: Like me! However, all of that has changed with this education. I have become more informed and will encourage everyone I meet to do likewise. The history books will have to change their perspective of us as passive, uninformed, uneducated voters to politically astute, active, and educated voters.

Dux: Yes, we can steadily increase the number of citizens who pay attention to such issues. Change is here from the grassroots level. I am excited to know what else will emerge!

Discipulus: Ooo la la. I will share this information with all my friends. Oh, how happy I am that I am empowered to make a significant difference!

Dux: As you know, members of Congress spend a lot of their time worrying about what their constituents think. These representatives realize their choices will be scrutinized in the future by their constituents and opponents. Hence, they try to anticipate their constituents' policy views. Legislators are more likely to act if they think their constituents will take them to task in the elections. As our country is a democracy, every citizen should have views and opinions on societal issues.

Discipulus: Can voters make such mega decisions?

Dux: Few Americans know much about politics. One major study showed only 25% of respondents could name two senators, only 29% could name their U.S. representatives, and fewer than 50% knew that the first ten Constitutional amendments are called the Bill of Rights.

Discipulus: All the more reason for this new political education awakening!

Dux: Taking the time to learn can seem daunting. Plus, people often think that their informed actions will rarely make much of a difference when compared to the cost of informing oneself. Therefore, it can sometimes seem rational to remain ignorant. A more moderate version of "rational ignorance" recognizes that some information is difficult to acquire. You see, becoming truly knowledgeable about politics requires substantial investments of time and energy. Many Americans seek to gain political knowledge cheaply and make political decisions by using shortcuts that seem to relieve them of engaging in information gathering and evaluation.

Discipulus: Well Dux, I am now engaged in information gathering and evaluation.

Dux: Indulge me for a moment. What do you think would be a good job description for a Senator and a U.S. House Representative?

Discipulus: Excellent interpersonal and communication skills, a love for the people, and a solid understanding of the political system.

Dux: That makes sense to me. Based on what you've learned so far, what do you believe is the maximum number of years a senator or representative should serve?

Discipulus: Hmm. Good question. I'm not too keen on that job for life perk as with the Supreme Court justices. With shifting demographics and community interests, I say they should only serve a maximum of 10 to 12 years. And that's probably pushing it...

Dux: As for the time an individual can serve, it's practically endless, although a single term is two years for the House and six years for the Senate.

Discipulus: What! Does that mean the U.S. has many tired politicians, and we need to make a difference in 2024? So, you mean to tell me a Senator can serve six terms, 36 years, and still run again?

Dux: And they certainly do. As of June 2021, here are the members of Congress who have served over 30 years:

Name	Political Party	State	Entered Congress	Years Served
Senator Patrick Leahy	Democrat	Vermont	1975	46
Senator Chuck Grassley	Republican	Iowa	1975	46
Senator Richard Shelby	Democrat turned Republican	Alabama	1979	35
Representative Don Young	Republican	Alaska	1973	48
Representative Marcy Kaptur	Democrat	Ohio	1983	38

Discipulus: That's more than triple the number of years I was thinking! I am from Alaska, and my wife is from Vermont. I am 30 years old and there has been so much change in my lifetime. Do you mean to tell me these guys served in Congress before I was born? How have these congressional members adapted to change?

Dux: That is an excellent question to ask Discipulus. Some think these long-serving congress members do not understand the real world because they've held public office for so long. They are seen as "career politicians" who might be responsible for the nation's current state, partisanship, and a lackluster economy. As a result, political analysts ask whether voters would prefer a candidate who has never served congress over a career politician. At least the 22nd Amendment states that the president only gets two terms, a total of eight years.

Discipulus: Well, I am thankful for that because sometimes four years is enough!

Discipulus: Now, what of this Constitution, and what is the big thing about it?

Dux: The U.S. Constitution is the foundational set of rules for the U.S. Also known as the law of the land, it dictates how the branches of the government function and the rights of citizens.

Discipulus: How does that relate to me?

Dux: The U.S. Constitution is the "rule book" for government, and as a citizen, you have a right to contest any action of the government and others through its laws.

Discipulus: Wow, I have that power? I need to have a thorough knowledge of this rule book.

Dux: Yes. Let me share the story of how this great document originated. It should help you understand

the power of leadership and dramatically increase
your expectations of politicians due to the courage,
persistence, and determination of ordinary citizens. I
will start at the Boston Tea Party!

Discipulus: How does tea relate to politics and the writing
of such an excellent document? We are a coffee-
drinking nation. Do you think there is an error, and it
should be the Boston Coffee Party?

Dux: Not quite. In the 1770s, tea was an extremely
important commodity for consumption and in
commerce. In 1773, the British government granted
the East India Company a monopoly on tea export to
the 13 American colonies. Not only did those in the
American colonies resent they were being taxed
without having any representation in the British
parliament, business owners who were becoming
profitable from tea smuggling wanted to protect their
financial interests. Hence the demonstrated opposition
and retaliation led by Samuel Adams was named the
Boston Tea Party of 1773.

Discipulus: One man had that bravery, yet 535
Congressional members can't even pass as a simple
bill! So, what did brave, courageous Samuel Adams do?

Dux: Strategy. He provoked the British government to
take action that would alienate its colonial supporters
in the New England colonies and paved the way for a
rebellion. The rebels boarded the ships docked at the
Boston Harbor that carried the British East India tea

and dumped it into the water. Adams and his followers continued to agitate the British into enacting several harsh reprisals.

Discipulus: Oh? Tell me more. It is getting exciting!

Dux: Within five months, the House of Commons (a branch of the British government) passed a series of acts that closed the port of Boston to commerce, changed the government of Massachusetts, and restricted movement to the West, further alienating the southern planters who depended on access to Western lands.

Discipulus: My goodness!

Dux: Now that is the Tea Party. The provocation and retaliation resulted in the 1774 First Continental Congress. This assembly of delegates from the colonies called for a total boycott of British goods, thus beginning the separation and independence from British rule. The Second Continental Congress resulted in the creation of both the Constitution and the Declaration of Independence.

Discipulus: Well, one thing indeed leads to another. We are not dumping tea anymore. We now are into dumping non-functional politicians! I wonder what will emerge in this great country... Let me put on the thinking caps of Founding Fathers Thomas Jefferson, Benjamin Franklin, Roger Sherman, John Adams, Robert Livingston, and Alexander Hamilton. I see self-liberation, economic empowerment, and freedom.

Dux: Now, how did you know of all those high-ranking
    founders?

Discipulus: Well, I had to remember something from high
    school! Did any of those Founding Fathers have
    anything to do with the Electoral College? I heard that
    there was a big toss-up in the 2000 general election,
    and there was a lot of buzz and confusion around the
    Electoral College. I thought elections ended after the
    election night votes were counted.

Dux: The U.S. Electoral College is a group of electors who
    elect the president and vice-president. When you vote
    for a presidential candidate, you are voting for electors
    who then cast their votes for the winning candidate of
    that state. Article II of the Constitution lists the
    specifics of the Electoral College. The Founding Fathers
    included the Electoral College as one of the famous
    "checks and balances" for two reasons: 1) to give
    states with small populations more equal weight in the
    presidential election and 2) they didn't trust the
    average citizen's competence to make an informed
    decision on the best choice for president. Remember,
    women couldn't vote.

Discipulus: This is becoming very complex. How are the
    votes determined?

Dux: The number of electoral votes per state is
    determined by adding the number of the state's
    senators and representatives together. For example,

California has 2 senators and 53 representatives;
hence they have 55 electoral votes. The single
exception is the District of Columbia, which has a
standard of three electors. The total number of
electoral votes across all states is 538 votes.

Discipulus: I'm still confused. I always thought whichever
candidate received the most votes on election night
won the presidency. How does the Electoral College
come into play?

Dux: A candidate must have 270 electoral votes to win the
election formally. If there is a tie in votes (269 to 269),
the House of Representatives decides the president
and the Senate selects the vice-president.

Discipulus: How are electors selected?

Dux: The political parties in each state choose the
candidates for electors.

Discipulus: So, you mean to tell me before the results of
the elections, each state has Democratic and
Republican sets of electors?

Dux: Correct. Based on which party's candidate wins that
state, that slate of state electors cast their votes. It is
the case for all states except Nebraska and Maine,
where the elector slate can be mixed.

Discipulus: Now I have homework to read how Nebraska
and Maine can have a mixed party elector slate.

Dux: Great! You do not have to, although I enjoy your
enthusiasm to learn even more.

Discipulus: Now, how exactly does it work when the
House of Representatives must step in to determine
the presidency? I imagine the chaos that could cause.
In these uncertain times, anything can occur, and
preparation is the best strategy.

Dux: Each state's House of Representative delegation gets
one vote. Since there are 50 states, that means there
are 50 votes. A majority of 26 votes is needed to
determine the president. The senators elect the vice-
president, with each senator having one vote. The
winner must receive the majority of 51 votes. The
president and vice-president are scheduled to be
sworn in on January 20.

Discipulus: Very interesting! If it were not for you, I would
think it is my vote alone that counts. Do you mean to
tell me I would have continued to be so misinformed?
Why did the founders take this approach?

Dux: When the Constitution was written, many people
knew little about government, politics, and
presidential elections. A large portion of people at the
time were farmers or lived in rural areas. Many of
them also could not read or write. Their interest was
earning a living and providing for their families, not
those running for elected office. Like it or not, the
Founding Fathers were not confident that the average

citizen could make the most informed choices for the highest offices. Hence the creation of the Electoral College.

Discipulus: It sounds very much like today, even though we are so much more educated and have increased our overall financial status.

Dux: Technically, the Constitution does not require the electors to vote for the candidates chosen by their state's popular vote. However, some states do set that requirement. Interestingly, throughout the history of presidential elections, some electors have voted for a different party's candidate. However, by tradition, the electors vote for the candidate chosen by their state.

Discipulus: Sounds like trouble!

Dux: Bear with me because my following explanation gets a little complex. Electors vote on the first Monday after the second Wednesday in December. Then Congress meets in a joint session at 1:00 pm on a date set by law to count the electoral vote. As president of the Senate, the vice-president presides over the process and announces the newly elected president and vice president.

Discipulus: Oh! So it was on January 6, 2021, during the session of counting the electoral votes the Capitol was stormed to prevent the declaration of the 2020 presidential election winner.

Dux: Yes, a very significant threat to the nation's democracy, where the ramifications are still unfolding. Now back to the vote count.

Discipulus: Wait a minute. You are telling me after ordinary citizens vote, whether in person or by mail-in ballot, one member of the Electoral College has the power to negate the voice of the majority?

Dux: When all the electoral votes are counted, the candidate with the most votes wins. In most cases, the candidate who wins the popular vote also wins in the Electoral College. However, this is not guaranteed. As recent as the 2016 elections, Donald Trump won the presidency through the Electoral College even though he lost the popular vote. Hillary Clinton received about 2.9 million more votes nationwide (2.1%). Yet Trump received 304 electoral votes versus Clinton's 227, even as two faithless electors defected from Trump and five deflected from Clinton.

Discipulus: It was surprising how individuals ensured that they voted in the 2020 elections. I think the numbers were around 160 million, the highest in U.S. history.

Dux: I sincerely hope high voter turnout is a new trend. However, many factors pushed those numbers, including high dissatisfaction with the prior administration and a pandemic that restricted individuals to their homes. The people must maintain political involvement and activism. Relevant and practical education is the key.

Discipulus: I keep thinking about this Electoral College. There needs to be a change quickly - no more ceremony. You never know with humans when they will deviate. Too much is at stake. There must be a change.

Warren Buffett is indeed right with his quote: "The smarter the journalists are, the better off society is. For

to a degree, people read the press to inform
themselves - and the better the teacher, the better the
student body." I must think for myself. I am happy that
I invested the time to learn from you, Dux. I have
enjoyed the journey.

Dux: That is why you must be an educated voter, so you
can ask the relevant questions to discover your best
options. You must not rely on the media. Media outlets
are a business and will cover what they want to create
a biased perspective for their favorites.

Discipulus: I suppose a campaign is like a job interview,
just that it lasts longer and a lot of money is spent to
get the electorate to know you.

Dux: That is the power of campaigning, and that may be
the only time you see a humble politician asking for
your vote.

Discipulus: Now that I am well educated on the basics, I
am going to be voting proud and strong in all elections.
It sounds like the Electoral College has served its
original purpose. Voters should have their votes
counted on an individual basis. People need to
advocate this. The days of the Electoral College are
long past. As a country with so many resources, talent,
diversity, and power, we have become so inert, non-
functional, and ineffective as individuals on these
political issues.

I'll remember a famous quote from President John F. Kennedy: "Ask not what your country can do for you, ask what you can do for your country!"

Dux: Some feel that partisanship is a challenge in getting things done. Everyone seems to be in a partisan frame of mind. Few want to go the bipartisan way.

Discipulus: I remember a few presidents promising bipartisanship. What happened to their promise? Did that ship sail?

Dux: Most presidents say the same thing. It is an intelligent way to secure success and leave a strong legacy. Look at former President George W. Bush. Did you know he had a good relationship with the Democrats as governor of Texas? Yet, look at the stormy seas he traveled in Washington D.C.

Discipulus: D.C. is a different "kettle of fish," and I guess presidents learn to survive very quickly!

Thanks for making this discussion short and sweet. Now I have to do some additional reading. Although we just went through a major election, the mid-terms are coming up – what a relentless cycle. I am so fired up now with politics. It is sweeter than I thought!!!

I will be like Supreme Court Justice Hugo Black, who always carried a copy of the Constitution. I am following in his footsteps to regard it as "the best document in the world" to guide a government "of the people, by the people, and for the people."

Dux: Hats off to you Discipulus! Did you know that the U.S. Constitution is the longest-lasting written Constitution in the world? Did you also know that Thomas Jefferson, a Founding Father, believed that the Constitution should be rewritten or revised every 19 years?

Discipulus: No. I would not have guessed that.

Dux: I now leave you with the preamble to the Constitution. It is your responsibility to read this entire document and the Declaration of Independence.

The Preamble of the U.S. Constitution
We the People of the United States, in Order to form a more perfect Union, establish Justice, insure domestic Tranquility, provide for the common defense, promote the general Welfare, and secure the Blessings of Liberty to ourselves and our Posterity, do ordain and establish this Constitution for the United States of America.

APPENDIX: PERSONAL POLITICAL WORKSHEET

Take an opportunity to research the following questions as a starting point in deepening your political astuteness.

- Who are your state's elected officials in the House of Representatives and the U.S. Senate?
- Who is currently serving on the Supreme Court?
- What is your favorite piece of historical and modern legislation?
- What is one legislation you would like to see passed?
- If you could experience a politician's life for one day, which political role would you like to experience and why?

Recommended Task:

Write to your political representative at the local, state, or federal level and request an opportunity to shadow their office for a day. The following few pages after the sample note are real-life examples of letters written to political officials and their responses.

Dear (Politician's Name):

My name is ______________, and I am requesting to shadow your office for one day. I recently read *From Whence We Came: A Fun Political Conversation* written by Juliette Adams and was very intrigued by the political process. I want a greater experience-based approach to learn about the political system, which I feel can be achieved through a shadowing opportunity. The experience will give me a greater understanding of the challenges and opportunities in the political process. It also will have a lasting impact on accountability for political leaders and any future consideration for elected office.

I look forward to your reply.

Yours sincerely,
Sender name

APPENDIX: LETTER WRITTEN TO REPRESENTATIVE ED ROYCE (CA)

June 21, 2017

P.O. Box 2143
Merrifield, VA 22116

Congressman Ed Royce,
Chairman of Foreign Affairs Committee
2310 Rayburn House Office Building
Washington D.C. 20515

Dear Rep. Royce:

As a Caribbean/Guyanese American, I graciously write amidst June's Caribbean American Heritage Month celebration. I extend thanks to you for your support and vote for H.R. 4939: United States-Caribbean Strategic Engagement Act of 2016. I am impressed and elated by the high level of bipartisan support this Bill harnessed both in the House and Senate. I think Alexander Hamilton, a most honored Caribbean American, would have been pleased. It also allows the U.S. Congress to reciprocate to the Caribbean, parts of his contributions to the U.S. including being a Founding Father and 1st U.S. Secretary of Treasury.

The United States-Caribbean Strategic Engagement Act demonstrates individual citizens' power to influence their government to act on their behalf and create win-win partnerships. This action is reminiscent of the creator of the Broadway musical "Hamilton," Lin Manuel Miranda's, presentation to Congress to address the economic crisis in Puerto Rico on March 15, 2016.

I dare say that H.R. 4939 carries a legacy for real-time enactment of Hamilton's legacy of a new sustainable financial system for the Caribbean. I trust that the excitement over the thought of a pair of Hamilton tickets can be transferred to this novel and exciting concept. Thus resulting in a Congressional interpretation of a signature legacy of Alexander Hamilton.

I trust the reports presented to Congress will be inclusive of a manifestation of such a new financial system. A system that will facilitate "economic development and increase regional diversification and global competitiveness."

Yours sincerely,

Juliette Adams
American University '16

"Tomorrow is today! **We are confronted with the fierce urgency of now**! There is such a thing as being too late. Procrastination is still the thief of time. Life often leaves us standing bare, naked, and dejected with a lost opportunity." - Dr. Martin Luther King Jr.

October 16, 2009

Mr. Arne Duncan
Secretary of Education,
US Department of Education
400 Maryland Avenue, SW
Washington D.C 20202

Dear Secretary Duncan:

This letter is an urgent appeal for your action to enact an overhaul of the U.S. educational system, which is supported by the Bill and Melinda Gates Foundation 2009 Annual Report. Hence my proactive approach to offering my consulting services as part of an action-oriented plan to initiate and implement such much-needed changes.

My boldness and sense of urgency originate from the CNN March 23, 2009 interview of Fareed Zakaria with Bill and Melinda Gates on the topic "Fixing the Education Business," and the looming 2010 socio-economic challenges facing the nation when 75 million baby boomers start to retire. My concern, sincere enthusiasm, and futuristic outlook are largely due to my native socio-cultural background where education was truly promoted as, "No Child Will Be Left Behind"

From Zakaria's CNN interview, I describe myself as a "Golden Age" teacher with experience from the Caribbean and the U.S. from the levels of Head Start to the 1st year of college including the Arts, Natural and Social Science.

In Zakaria's interview, Melinda Gates clearly pinpointed the education challenge. The educational system, with its 65 million public school students, must be made applicable to the Information Age. Presently it is outdated and modeled after the Industrial Age, an issue that has been reiterated by Robert Kiyosaki in *Retire Young, Retire Rich* and highly supported by Napoleon Hill's 1937 golden book *Think and Grow Rich.*

Urgency has forced our nation to enact a "Blue Ocean Strategy." It is an approach used by Captain D. Michael Abrashoff as shared in his book, *It's Your Ship.* He outlined that innovation, risk techniques, and the belief in a high performing team to improve efficiency and the quality of sailors' lives brought the ship "Benfold" to a superior performance level and earned the accolades as the best ship in the Navy.

I am sure you understand the Gates Foundation's concerns amidst its optimism. If action is taken immediately, optimism prevails. However, if "business continues as usual," then indeed their apprehensiveness will be validated. I am confident that you believe in a relevant education system that empowers a student to be independent, mature, and have the skill to recognize opportunities so they can take care of themselves.

Hence, I am requesting a meeting with you at your earliest opportunity to make an in-person presentation.

Looking forward to your expedited response.

Yours sincerely,

Juliette Adams
Project Management Consultant

TOM DAVIS, VIRGINIA,
CHAIRMAN

CHRISTOPHER SHAYS, CONNECTICUT
DAN BURTON, INDIANA
ILEANA ROS-LEHTINEN, FLORIDA
JOHN M. McHUGH, NEW YORK
JOHN L. MICA, FLORIDA
GIL GUTKNECHT, MINNESOTA
MARK E. SOUDER, INDIANA
STEVEN C. LATOURETTE, OHIO
TODD RUSSELL PLATTS, PENNSYLVANIA
CHRIS CANNON, UTAH
JOHN J. DUNCAN, JR., TENNESSEE
CANDICE MILLER, MICHIGAN
MICHAEL R. TURNER, OHIO
DARRELL ISSA, CALIFORNIA
VIRGINIA BROWN-WAITE, FLORIDA
JON C. PORTER, NEVADA
KENNY MARCHANT, TEXAS
LYNN A. WESTMORELAND, GEORGIA
PATRICK T. McHENRY, NORTH CAROLINA
CHARLES W. DENT, PENNSYLVANIA
VIRGINIA FOXX, NORTH CAROLINA

ONE HUNDRED NINTH CONGRESS

Congress of the United States
House of Representatives

COMMITTEE ON GOVERNMENT REFORM

2157 RAYBURN HOUSE OFFICE BUILDING

WASHINGTON, DC 20515–6143

MAJORITY (202) 225-5074
FACSIMILE (202) 225-3974
MINORITY (202) 225-5051
TTY (202) 225-6852

http://reform.house.gov

HENRY A. WAXMAN, CALIFORNIA,
RANKING MINORITY MEMBER

TOM LANTOS, CALIFORNIA
MAJOR R. OWENS, NEW YORK
EDOLPHUS TOWNS, NEW YORK
PAUL E. KANJORSKI, PENNSYLVANIA
CAROLYN B. MALONEY, NEW YORK
ELIJAH E. CUMMINGS, MARYLAND
DENNIS J. KUCINICH, OHIO
DANNY K. DAVIS, ILLINOIS
WM. LACY CLAY, MISSOURI
DIANE E. WATSON, CALIFORNIA
STEPHEN F. LYNCH, MASSACHUSETTS
CHRIS VAN HOLLEN, MARYLAND
LINDA T. SANCHEZ, CALIFORNIA
C.A. DUTCH RUPPERSBERGER,
    MARYLAND
BRIAN HIGGINS, NEW YORK
ELEANOR HOLMES NORTON,
    DISTRICT OF COLUMBIA

BERNARD SANDERS, VERMONT
    INDEPENDENT

July 1, 2005

Ms. Juliette Adams
Caribbean Diaspora Empowerment Foundation
PO Box 904
Greenbelt, MD 20768

Dear Ms. Adams:

Thank you for writing to express your support for H. Con. Res. 171, which would establish a Caribbean American Heritage Month. It is my sincere pleasure to inform you that this resolution was adopted by the House of Representatives this past Monday, June 27. The resolution was received by the Senate and now awaits consideration by the Committee on the Judiciary. Thank you again for your correspondence and support of this measure.

Sincerely,

Tom Davis
Chairman

An election campaign is an organized activity where candidates present their ideas and positions to voters over an extended period, in support of their candidacy for elected office. A good campaign assists voters in making educated voting decisions. To be effective, the candidate's message must be clear and consistent, and use many mediums to deliver their message, including traditional media and social media. Although primarily focused on their own message, a candidate may seek to get their opponents to go "off-message" by deviating from their key points.

Some of the tools used to build a campaign and reinforce a candidate's message are media advisories, message boxes, a message calendar, news stories, op-eds, press releases, speeches, and talking points.

- Media advisory: An invitation to media outlets to cover an upcoming campaign event.
- Message box: A visual representation of the message landscape on a particular issue showing the contrast between the positions of a candidate and their opponent.

Message Box Template

Candidate on Candidate	Candidate on Opponent
• Positive Views • Proponent Views	• Negative • Proponent Views
Opponent on Candidate	Opponent on Opponent
• Negative Views • Opponent Views	• Positive Views • Opponent Views

- Message calendar: A calendar populated with significant dates and events to guide media posts and communications.

- News story: A written or recorded article or interview that informs the public about current events, concerns, or ideas. It is also a source of cheap, immediate coverage.

- Op-ed: Formally known as "opposite the editorial page," an op-ed is a published opinion to educate an audience and generate thought and discussion among readers.

- Press release: An official statement to media outlets to generate news and arouse public interest.

- Speeches: A persuasive tool to arouse interest, influence, and gain trust through delivering ideology and positions on issues.

- Talking points: Straightforward, short statements that outline candidate's policies and ideas. They enable the candidate to direct discussions on issues and are a point of reference in speeches, interviews, and other conversations.

The following documents were created in 2016 for the Robert Portman 2016 Ohio Senate race campaign as part of a Master of Science program. The final election was between incumbent Senator Robert Portman (R) and Democratic challenger Ted Strickland (D). In the Democratic primary for the Senate race, Alexander Paul George (P.G.) Sittenfeld ran against Ted Strickland.

It was a closely contested race that pollsters called a statistical tie. Senator Portman, a strong advocate for drug rehabilitation, gun rights, fair international trade deals, and fiscal responsibility, was accused of being out of touch with the Ohioans and not the job creator the state needed. Although Strickland favored equality of America in trade arrangements, as with the Trans-Pacific Partnership, he was accused of costing the state a high number of jobs as governor. Portman (R) ultimately won the 2016 election. However, he has declined to run for reelection in 2022.

Campaign Message	
Community Empowerment is essential in assisting the development of strong families. Awareness in one's community also serves as a security control.	
Day of the Week	**Outlined Activities and Communications**
Saturday	<ul><li>Fighting for Jobs and Family Outdoor event with vendors from the business and nonprofit community</li><li>Press Release: Fighting for Jobs and Family Outdoor event</li><li>Media Advisory: Political Jeopardy family event</li><li>Launch Community Empowerment Ad</li></ul>
Sunday	<ul><li>Community barbeque with vendors throughout the state</li><li>Press release: Community Barbeque</li><li>Media Advisory on Community Conversation on "the New American"</li><li>Launch Community Empowerment Ad</li></ul>
Monday	<ul><li>Political Jeopardy family event focusing on the tremendous contributions of individuals in American History, including Alexander Hamilton, Benjamin Franklin, and George Washington</li><li>Press Release: Political Jeopardy Family Event</li><li>Media Advisory: French City Chili Fest</li><li>Launch Community Empowerment Ad</li></ul>

Tuesday	<ul><li>Conversation on "the New American"</li><li>Press Release: "New American" - Focus on the importance of citizenship using Theodore Roosevelt's speech "Citizenship in a Republic."</li><li>Medial Advisory: Senior Citizens Appreciation Day</li><li>Launch Community Empowerment Ad</li></ul>
Wednesday	<ul><li>Participation at the French Chili Fest interacting with the general public</li><li>Press release: French Chili Fest</li><li>Media Advisory: Mother and daughter event</li><li>Launch Community Empowerment Ad</li></ul>
Thursday	<ul><li>Visit three neighborhood senior citizens homes</li><li>Press release: Visit to senior citizens' homes as a form of appreciation for their contribution to society</li><li>Media Advisory on Soccer Game Kick Off</li><li>Launch Community Empowerment Ad</li></ul>
Friday	<ul><li>Mother and daughter event: Importance of family relations and contributions of women and children</li><li>Press Release: Mother and Daughter Event</li><li>Media advisory: Interfaith Service attendance</li><li>Launch of Community Empowerment Ad</li></ul>

Media Advisory   Contact: Blessings Goodman
February 27, 2016   Phone: 740-720-1007

Sen. Robert Portman to host a Town Hall meeting to
discuss International Trade (IT)
The event is to determine the needs of Millennials as an
economic catalyst for IT.

CAMBRIDGE, Ohio – Sen. Robert Portman invites all
emerging entrepreneurs, specifically Millennials,
interested in international trade to Ohio University on
February 27, 2016. He will have a candid exchange on
"International Trade as a Job Creator for the Local
Business Community - Increasing the Effectiveness of
Washington's Small Business Administration (SBA)."

Portman is enthusiastic that the meeting composition will
be a predominately Millennial audience. This event allows
him to present international trade as a job builder and
better understand Millennials' needs through discussion
and feedback. He understands the importance of
connecting with this unique and dynamic generational
group on the economic disparities present in achieving the
"American Dream." As an international trade expert, he is
adamant about rapidly creating jobs and rebuilding the
middle class by accessing untapped global markets.

Who: Senator Robert Portman
What: Boosting job creation for Millennials and reducing
economic disparities through IT

Where: Ohio State University, Bennett Hall
Chillicothe, OH 45601
When: Saturday, February 27, 2016, at noon.
Why: Increasing small business success rates as an economic empowerment strategy for decreasing economic disparities.

###

News Source and Reporter Names:
1) Morning Consult - Reid Wilson
2) The Columbus Dispatch - Michele Everhart
3) The Washington Post - Chris Cillizza
4) Geo Engineering Watch - Dane Wigington
5) The Huffing Post - Christina Wilkie

To be used by a surrogate on his behalf.

Trade: Senator Robert Portman, the Republican incumbent in the Ohio Senate race, places substantial value on community recreational activities. As a widely traveled individual and U.S. trade representative with experience in the international community, he recognizes the power of community in reducing fears of other cultures and nationalities.

Senator Portman advocates for more substantial international trade agreements, creating win-win situations where Americans' jobs and salaries would not be comprised. Increased exports can contribute to the reduction of the large deficit the U.S. has with China.

Senator Portman seeks to build on established trade agreements, ensuring profitability through exercising greater accountability and oversight. An example is the congressional approved African Growth Opportunity Act (AGOA).

Small Business: Small businesses have always received great respect from Senator Portman. He recognizes them as an economic driver and booster for the U.S. With U.S. debt at $18 trillion, he advocates making small businesses more viable and successful. Senator Portman supports increased community-based programs hosted by small businesses.

Drug Reform: Senator Portman understands the
importance of community support and firmly believes
that every person must be given the best chance,
despite the vices available within society. Hence, he
was responsible for two congressional bills, the Drug-
Free Communities Act and the Comprehensive
Addiction and Recovery Act.

Foreign Relations: Senator Portman understands the value
of stronger foreign and trade relations. His experience
as a U.S. trade representative has been extremely
valuable in building strong international relationships
through business, which ultimately fosters more
significant ties in the global fight against terrorism.

Fiscal Responsibility: Senator Portman has served as
Director of the Office Management and Budget.
Additionally, national security has always been of
great interest to him. He understands the impact and
causal relationship between the security of a nation
and its economy.

Terrorism: As an informed member of Congress, Senator
Portman recognizes that terrorism is both
transnational and domestic. Senator Portman
understands the challenges of transnational terrorism
in the international community and its high cost.
Therefore, he seeks alternative proactive non–military
interventions, including Countering Violent Extremism
(CVE).

Education: Senator Portman recognizes the emergence of a new generation – "the Millennials." He believes the education system must be adjusted to meet their needs. He advocates for greater state control through a pilot program with measurable variables.

Immigration: Senator Portman's international and trade experience has provided him with an understanding of the importance of solving the national immigration problem. He has an initial plan to control the entry and exit of individuals.

Veterans: Senator Portman recognizes that veterans have been neglected over the past decades and must be respected. He supports the country's responsibility to veterans when they return from military service. Understanding that jobs are essential, he has incentives to involve veterans in international trade, using their experience and knowledge in the countries where they fought and were stationed.

Second Amendment: Senator Portman strongly supports the Second Amendment "the right of the people to keep and bear arms... shall not be infringed." Hence, he advocates for more investment in mental health issues to prevent incorrect gun use.

Portman On Portman	Portman On Sittenfeld
Candidate on Candidate: Positive Views, Candidate Views	*Candidate on Opponent: Negative Views, Candidate Views*
• Pro-growth job plan: An active proponent for "Jobs for America" and the Senate Republican Plan for Creating Jobs and Prosperity. • Promoter of international trade: Was the 14th United States Trade Representative and a strong advocate for free and fair trade. • Government Fiscal Responsibility: 35th Director of the Office Management and Budget. A strong advocate for a balanced budget. • Promotion of rehabilitation program for drug abuse: Has 20+ years of experience – an important issue due to the state's increased drug use.	• Inexperience in dealing with the challenges and responsibilities of the Senate: Only 5 years experience as a council member and a political career that began in 2011. • Against job growth and economic stimulus: Strong opponent against the Keystone XL pipeline project. • Lack of fiscal policy understanding: Wants large banks to split their commercial and investment practices. • Won't protect gun rights as outlined by the Second Amendment: Has the misguided belief that merely the possession of guns causes mass murders and not the larger issues of

Authored Drug-Free Communities Act and the Comprehensive Addiction and Recovery Act. • Enhanced Veteran Service: Greater advocacy for transition programs from the military to civilian status and better military benefits.	mental illness and radicalism. • Consistent flip-flopper: Key example -campaigned against streetcars, but now is for them.

For Immediate Release
February 12, 2016

Contact: Blessings Goodman
Phone: 740-720-1039

Sen. Robert Portman establishes a community focus group to assist in the development of a community intervention strategic plan addressing terrorism

Cambridge, OH - Senator Portman and his national security campaign team met with over 1,000 attendees at Ohio University to discuss the issue of terrorism and establish a community focus group to create a proactive strategic plan. It was a challenging meeting, as it involved presenting the complex topic of terrorism and the significant impact community intervention can have.

On entering the meeting room, attendees were greeted with the song, "Waging War" by CeCe Winans. "*Anoint my head, anoint my feet. Send your angels raining down, here on the battle ground. For your glory were taking territory, fighting unseen enemies, like never before. We are raging war.*" These words set the tone that communities can significantly reduce or eliminate threats while maintaining freedom and liberty.

Sen. Portman stated that one of the significant reasons Congress' public approval continues to be below 20% is its lackluster efforts in building a strong community partnership, even though promises of improvement are made continuously. Hence, he resolved to take a stance in addressing the community intervention initiative. "Terrorists come from the community. Their greatest source of support is the community, and in many cases, their continued existence is from their communities," stated Senator Portman. Terrorism has even greater significance to the U.S. community due to the increased recruitment of foreign fighters.

One attendee who volunteered for the focus group stated that she was delighted terrorism was being addressed from a community and solution-oriented level. Especially as major media outlets primarily provide horrific images and gruesome information, which can leave individuals in hopelessness and fear, she expressed great satisfaction in learning about the security avenues that communities can proactively use while maintaining liberties and freedom.

One millennial in attendance also stated that this meeting was representative of the level of creativity and "out of the box" thinking he expects from political leaders. "Some of the national solutions lie in the community where freedom and liberty are very important." He shared his great astonishment that many liberties are being reduced in the name of security. Yet, individuals have greater access to advanced technology, which can threaten their fellow citizens. Reverberating amongst the crowd as they left were the words of "Waging War," "*I'm ready for the battle, I'm ready to win. My weapon of power. He lives within.*"

The strategic plan will be presented at a community follow-up meeting on Saturday, March 27, 2016, at the University of Ohio.

The Closely Contested Ohio Senate Race of Portman and Strickland Focuses on Commitment

Cleveland, OH – The U.S. presidential campaign has dramatically extended its influence on the Ohio Senate race, as presidential hopeful, Gov. John Kasich from Ohio, is endorsed by Senator Robert Portman. Portman is running for reelection to the Senate against the winner of the Democratic primary, which will either be Ted Strickland or P.G. Sittenfeld. Although many social, political, and economic issues are being addressed in the local Senate race, voters are quite interested to know which presidential candidate has the most significant support in the state and who will win the nomination.

There is a need for an independent-minded representative with a bipartisan perspective to end stalemates and achieve effective congressional action. Greater emphasis is needed to ensure that trade deals are negotiated in the U.S. interest and address the concern of jobs continuously being shipped abroad, depriving the general population of opportunities to earn a fair wage. Therefore, an international trade agreement must increase the number of high-quality jobs in the state. Local initiatives for job creation can take the form of increasing tourism. Increasing town hall meetings would maintain an open dialogue with the community. Also, a semi-annual survey could be sent out to citizens.

A clear message from Gov. Kasich's campaign is the large number of jobs created and regained that have economically stimulated the development of the state. John from the Experience Columbus Visitor's Center cited the variety of stable job opportunities in Columbus. However, there is significant uncertainty of the two Democratic candidates' positions on national security, as they have been accused of refusing a public debate on the issue. P.G Sittenfeld has admonished Strickland for refusing a debate on national security. Strickland claims he has to focus on his senatorial rival Robert Portman. It is a weak argument for Ohio's former governor and a candidate who previously served in the House of Representatives. These experiences should have contributed to a strong understanding of the challenges and issues in national security. In addition, the debate would have served as an ideal opportunity to show the perceived incompetence and lack of experience of Sittenfeld, the councilman from Cleveland.

The issue of jobs is a very contentious subject because Portman held a very senior position as a U.S. trade representative under the Bush Administration. He has been accused of creating massive debt as it relates to China. He thus needs to position himself as a job creator, especially as citizens question whether an increase of jobs would be a short-term phenomenon or a continuous trend in the entire state. As Jenna from Bowling Green Visitors Center stated, tertiary education must be high quality. There needs to be an adjustment to the educational system to emphasize trade and skills to meet the demands of the market. There is also a greater call for diplomacy and collaboration with other nations. Portman and Sittenfeld need to understand the needs of Millennials, who are very creative and dynamic in their thinking. Strong advocacy at the federal level would accommodate the emerging creativity of the Millennials.

Overall, the country's direction is of great concern, as Ohioans understand their state's economic viability and performance is connected to the nation's wellbeing. Republicans are particularly concerned about the below performance in the voting history of Strickland. They recognize that one's voting history is indicative of their commitment. As a U.S. congressman in 1993-1994 and 1997-2006, Strickland missed 5% of his votes, above the average for Congressional members. It is especially important as Congress's national rating is below 20%. There is great concern regarding his ability to represent his state and facilitate any well-needed change to Congressional culture.

Robert Portman
"Putting experience on your side"
University of Ohio
Athens, Ohio
August 31, 2016

I, Robert Portman, was raised in Cincinnati and am a truly dedicated citizen of Ohio. Today, I will tell you why I am a great Ohioan senatorial candidate. Apart from understanding the average Ohioan, I have worked at various governmental levels, including as a U.S. Trade Representative, Director of the Office Management and Budget, a congressman in the House of Representatives, and now as your Senator.

I am a fierce proponent of the community because a strong community brings opportunities for economic prosperity and a strong sense of security. Feeling you are a part of your community gives a strong sense of independence and confidence. So, I encourage security companies to be involved and visible in the community.

Even though I am portrayed as a Washington insider, that is a false assertion because I am working on your behalf. You must understand that there are 99 other Senators, all of whom have influence over the legislative procedure to get bills passed. Again, I stress that my purpose and objective is working in the interest of Ohioans.

As you all know, I am widely traveled both personally and in my professional capacity as U.S. Trade Representative. In my travels, I have experienced humbling interactions with people of various cultures. These experiences lend to my understanding and greater appreciation for Ohio as a diverse state. My increased cultural sensitivity gives me the confidence that together, we will find the solutions regardless of how difficult the challenges.

One recent issue I have confronted from my opponents is the accusation that I "flip-flopped" on trade deals, the latest being the Trans-Pacific Partnership (TPP), which is marketed with the projected objective to increase "Made in America" exports, grow the American economy, support well-paying American jobs, and strengthen the middle class. My opponents have labeled me an opportunist Senator because I now do not support this trade deal. My dear friends, the ultimate goal is to do the best for Ohioans and the country as a whole. With experience, you will understand that there are times when one can take a position, then realize at the last moment, it was not the best position. I am courageous and humble enough to reconsider objective information and change my position for the benefit of you, my constituency.

To reiterate my passion for strengthening communities, I am a strong advocate against human trafficking. I have authored five bills, including the Human Trafficking Act. I know you all agree that slavery created a tremendous toll on our community, resulting in significant psychological after-effects and economic challenges present in today's society. The psychological and economic dangers of human trafficking threaten to accelerate the moral decay of society and destroy the social fabric necessary for the prosperity of all citizens.

Citizens of Cleveland, Columbus, Cincinnati, and all other cities in Ohio, I am your leader for today and tomorrow. For you younger citizens, I strive to understand your dynamic thinking, your love for change, and the knowledge of knowing that you are important in a significant way. Hence, I developed a business team model called the "Millennials Challenge" which was comprised of eight leaders advising me on a strategic business initiative to invigorate and excite the Millennial community. I encourage your contributions and feedback because I learn from you about your true needs. I am from the baby boomer generation, which embraces stability and a fixed environment. However, I understand your differences and have made adjustments to have a win-win partnership here in Ohio.

Winston Churchill, the famous British Prime Minister credited for winning World War II, once said: "Americans try everything before trying the right thing." However, in my second term, I take up Churchill in his words that "I am the optimist who sees the opportunity in every difficulty." As the dawning of 2017 comes, we will rise with newness and great creativity to meet the challenges of the 21st century.

Liberty Enhances Security: It Must Be Preserved

Benjamin Franklin once said, "They who can give up essential liberty to obtain a little temporary safety deserve neither liberty or safety." Is the nation at this point? 2016 U.S. presidential candidate Donald Trump recommended a temporary ban for Muslims migrating to the U.S. Trump's statements demonstrated the extreme measures government could employ on behalf of security. At the same time, Franklin cautions citizens of the imminent adverse effects when liberty is sacrificed for temporary protection. Both statements call on citizens to become more involved in policies, regulations, and programs to reduce the significant shift of lessened liberty for greater security in a democracy. Greater citizen activism must demand elected officials show excellence, prosperity maintenance, and robust community relations.

Citizens demanding political excellence must require their political leaders to exercise creativity and innovation, so there are minimal restrictions of liberty in the event of a security-related issue. An effective way is to demand consistent communication with political leaders and develop a strong partnership based on trust. Partnership lends to citizens becoming community guardians by exercising their freedom of speech, religion, and assembly. Hence, if there is a significant threat of crime or terrorism, community involvement can be automatically triggered, which ultimately reduces law enforcement involvement.

The economic system in a democracy is a free market that promotes productivity, international competitiveness, and prosperity. However, there must be maximum liberty to thrive in such a free market since citizens are the "engines." When a government takes action to reduce freedom under the guise of security, the society can quickly transcend into an oligarchy where a few hold power over the majority. Such a form of government lends to a volatile environment of violence, prompting the government to resort to a militarized state of law and order for security, and significant reductions in liberties and economic activity.

As the US is the premier advocate for global democracy, fostering and maintaining international relations is extremely important. However, due to the country's increasing demographic diversity, the role of liberty in enhancing positive relationships becomes even more important. These relationships extend into the international community, which can visualize the relation-building in their communities. Celebrating diversity contributes to greater prosperity and an environment where community members feel free to build their commonality, bridge gaps, and reduce and resolve conflicts. This is an important issue, particularly for the Muslim immigrant community, as Muslims and Islam have become synonymous with terrorism. For example, Islamic groups should have promptly convened a town hall forum with the 2016 presidential candidates, the general public, and major news outlets to resolve the proposed temporary ban on Muslims immigrating to the U.S. Such an action could have reduced existing tensions.

It has been demonstrated that liberty, in conjunction with trusted relationships with political leaders, enhances security and a thriving economy. Therefore, liberty does not have to be significantly reduced in a threatening environment. It can enhance security where there is trust between political leaders and the community, outstanding political leadership, and economic freedoms. However, the primary onus is upon citizens to ensure they elect exemplary qualified individuals to the respective political office, so enhanced security is not used as a ploy to reduce citizens' liberty. Informed political decisions thus helps to ensure the appropriate balance between civil rights and security is maintained.

REFERENCES

About Us. Retrieved from International Institute for
   Democracy and Electoral Assistance (n.d.):
   https://www.idea.int/about-us

Beckwith, D. C. (2017, February 2). *United States
   Presidential Election of 2016.* Retrieved from
   Britannica:
   https://www.britannica.com/topic/United-States-
   presidential-election-of-2016

Berger, M. (2021, November 22). *U.S. listed as a
   'backsliding' democracy for first time in report by
   European think tank.* Retrieved from The
   Washington Post:
   https://www.washingtonpost.com/world/2021/1
   1/22/united-states-backsliding-democracies-list-
   first-time/

Delli, M., & Keeter, S. (1996). *What Americans Know About
   Politics and Why it Matters.* New Haven: Yale
   University Press

Electoral College: About the electors. (2021, May 5).
   Retrieved from National Archives:
   https://www.archives.gov/electoral-
   college/electors

Gallup. (2021, May 26). *Satisfaction With the United
   States.* Gallup.com.
   https://news.gallup.com/poll/1669/general-
   mood-country.aspx.

History.com Editors. (2020, September 25). *Boston Tea Party*. Retrieved from HISTORY: https://www.history.com/topics/american-revolution/boston-tea-party

Jones, J. M. (2021, April 3). *GOP Image Slides Giving Democrats Strong Advantage*. Gallup.com. https://news.gallup.com/poll/329561/gop-image-slides-giving-democrats-strong-advantage.aspx.

Statistics and Historical Comparison: Bills by Final Status. Retrieved from GovTrack (n.d.): https://www.govtrack.us/congress/bills/statistics

Juliette Adams is a native of Guyana, an oil-producing country in the Amazon basin with a dual Caribbean and South American identity. Her Guyanese identity and CLASS training (a quality measurement assessment examining teacher/student interaction) contribute to a comprehensive understanding of the grassroots machinery to assist the average citizen in bridging gaps and navigating political systems. She is a relentless advocate of autonomy, trust, objectivity, education, and the belief that the U.S. political system works for the politically educated and courageous participant.

From volunteering with local and national campaigns to lobbying Congress for African, Caribbean, and Israeli legislation, Juliette Adams' experience with the U.S. political system has been diverse, explorative, and bipartisan. Her non-governmental experiences encompass being a member of the World Bank Group Civil Society Policy Forum (WBG, CSPF), providing advisory service on an Argentinean women's initiative, and pioneering a "Chat Time" discussion series on Caribbean economic development at the Embassy of Guyana in the Kalorama neighborhood of Washington D.C.

As a culturally proficient professional, Adams' extensive teaching experience in the Caribbean and US allows her to simplify complex ideas and connect abstract concepts to everyday experience. Her classroom expertise coupled with degrees from Howard University in Business Administration and American University in Justice, Law,

and Society translates into a passion for empowering
individuals to contribute constructive change through
action.

The Gifted & Magical 95 Percent series is a five-book mini-series designed to help readers navigate a complex political system. It combines Juliette's political acumen with cumulative insight from her varied teaching experiences to examine drivers of human behaviors and generate action-based thought. As an extension, The Frederick Press is a platform to promote dynamic analysis through a Gifted & Magical framework: www.thefrederickpress.com. Both ventures advance adult critical thinking and promote a deeper understanding of concepts through analysis and reasoning.

You are invited to engage in a culturally safe and diverse global community and help generate consistent advocacy in the national political-economic equity fight.